Renewal Reminders

Renewal Reminders

David Haney
and James Mahoney

Broadman Press
Nashville, Tennessee

4251-62
ISBN: 0-8054-5162-5

Dewey Decimal Classification: 242
Subject headings: MEDITATIONS // CHRISTIAN LIFE
Library of Congress Catalog Card Number: 77-86310
Printed in the United States of America

Credits

Foreword

The words *renewal* and *reminder* go together. In the Bible, when the word *renew* is used, it refers to the "mind," the attitude or the spirit with which we live and do. For instance, in the Old Testament: "Create in me a clean heart, O God; and renew a right spirit within me" (Ps. 51:10). And, in the New Testament: "Be not conformed to this world: but be ye transformed by the renewing of your mind, that ye may prove what is that good, and acceptable, and perfect, will of God" (Rom. 12:2). Truly, they go together!

The next question has to do with how you can use these short essays. One, you may use them for daily devotional thoughts. Or, two, you may use them as the seeds for devotions and sermons. Or, both!

These renewal reminders come from messages and articles the two of us have preached and shared across the United States and Europe in renewal and deeper-life conferences, in our pastorates, and in other churches.

Our journey together goes back to the early sixties when our Lord allowed us to pastor neighboring churches in Dayton, Ohio. Our mutual affirmation has been rewarding, but not "beyond words": these RENEWAL REMINDERS are evidence of that!

DAVID P. HANEY
AND
JAMES MAHONEY

Contents

Renewal Reminders

1. Every Composer Is at the Mercy of His Interpreters

We must be regarded as Christ's subordinates and as stewards of the secrets of God. Well then, stewards are expected to show themselves trustworthy (1 Cor. 4:1–2, NEB).

It is true that every composer is at the mercy of his interpreters. Imagine, if you will, a beginning piano student, with chubby fingers and an absence of any semblance of rhythm, crashing and flailing away at Beethoven and upon completion saying, "That's Beethoven!" But, that's not Beethoven!

Imagine, then a cultured pianist, with years of training and an abundance of native ability, sitting down behind the same piece. Now, that's Beethoven!

Every Composer Is at the Mercy of His Interpreters!

So, too, our Lord!

The Word became flesh and the Word wrote the life in living letters as it was intended to be played. In him was man, not mere Homo sapiens, but man the *imago dei*—in the "image of God."

Graciously, then, he set the piece before us to play, also. We become . . . Christ-ians. But alas, we hit at the notes, striking as many discords as chords—in act, word, thought, and deed. And, then, with the audacity so natural, yet so unbecoming of us, we say, "That's Christ!" But, that's not Christ!

Every composer, even Christ, is at the mercy of his interpreters!

Ought it not, then, to behoove us to practice a bit before performance? Perhaps to get ourselves "in tune" and "in time"?

Then it will not be we who say, "That's Christ!" Others will!

And, that's what really counts, isn't it?

Renewal Reminder: *Remind me, O Lord, as trite as it sounds, to let others see you in me today. Amen.*

NOTES:

2. What a Ridiculous Rhyme!

We can make a large horse turn around and go wherever we want by means of a small bit in his mouth. And a tiny rudder makes a huge ship turn wherever the pilot wants it to go, even though the winds are strong. So also the tongue is a small thing, but what enormous damage it can do. A great forest can be set on fire by one tiny spark. Sometimes it praises our heavenly Father, and sometimes it breaks out into curses against men who are made like God. And so blessing and cursing come pouring out of the same mouth. Dear brothers, surely this is not right! (Jas. 3:3–5, 9–10, TLB).

"Sticks and stones may break my bones,
But words will never hurt me!"

Of all the quaint little rhymes that manage repetition from generation to generation, this is surely one of the most ridiculous.

Sticks and stones may bruise the body. But as weapons, they are nursery toys compared to the lethal power of words. Words wound deep; they cut a deep gash and leave scars for life! Words can cut to the bone—rather, they cut to the heart! From some lips they fall with the savage, slashing effect of a saber.

With rapier effect, words can be used unmercifully, indefensibly, in a salacious and scandalous attack. Or more subtly, just the drop of a remark can rip the sensitive heart like a razor!

Therefore, I always tremble when words are exchanged too freely among church members. It would be less dangerous if two people stood and began throwing daggers at one another!

Alas, there is an evil bent in the nature of us all which responds to the "call of the wild!" Yes, and the tongue is toughest to tame.

Consequently, gracious speech is a hallmark of spiritual maturity:

"For in many things we offend all. If any man offend not in word, the same is a perfect man, and able to bridle the whole body" (Jas. 3:2).

How soothing and healing and comforting are the words from heavenly lips—that kind word of encouragement, that whispered prayer, that request for forgiveness, that compliment sincerely spoken. Send me no flowers and give me no gift—but, oh, please tell me, "I love you."

Renewal Reminder: *Remind me, O Lord, to say unto others as I would have others say unto me. Amen.*

NOTES:

3. Does God Ever Grade on a Curve?

For we have not an high priest which cannot be touched with the feeling of our infirmities; but was in all points tempted like as we are, yet without sin. Let us therefore come boldly unto the throne of grace, that we may obtain mercy, and find grace to help in time of need (Heb. 4:15–16).

"Grading on the curve" is a familiar term to high school and college students. The teacher makes a list of all the class scores, then plots a "curve" to determine which students will fall in the A category, the B category, the C range, and the lowly brackets of D and F.

God occasionally grades on a curve. It might sound surprising, but it should certainly be understood that God judges us, giving due consideration to our emotional curve.

Everyone of us has an emotional curve. It's called by a fancy name, a cyclothymic curve. When emotions are up, we feel great, but when emotions are down, we have the blahs. Sometimes we feel like a moon shot; later we feel like a sick oyster at the low tide. But it is little realized that everyone's emotions will go up and down in cycles every few weeks, or every few months, depending upon the person. If you are willing to take the trouble, you could almost chart a person's curve and avoid him on his bad days, when unusual crises cut through to alter or reverse the cycle.

Expect it, dear Christian! Our emotional nature will go through its cycle from glum to glow. One's emotions are never tranquil, steady, or constantly serene. We have emotional ups and downs, and God "[knows] my downsitting and mine uprising" (Ps. 139:2).

God always knows just how we feel! He is patiently understanding with our shallow living during times of emotional low tide. He knows the ebb tide hampers us, yet he never pampers us, but expects a performance commensurate with our possibilities at the moment!

Yes, in one sense, God grades on the curve!

Renewal Reminder: *Remind me, O Lord, that*

you always operate at room temperature even when I'm hot or cold. Amen.

NOTES:

4.   A Jumbo Weekend

Fear not, little flock; for it is your Father's good pleasure to give you the kingdom (Luke 12:32).

It was one of the most unusual weekends I have ever had. It started when Etienne picked me up in front of my hotel in Zurich, Switzerland, bound for a weekend retreat in the Zurich Oberlands.

They called it a "Jumbo Weekend" and they held it twice each year, spring and autumn. It had started several years before.

A small, weekly Bible study/prayer-sharing group had been started in Zurich by members of a Baptist church. It grew, and because the size became a problem for participation they decided to divide it.

But it grew again. And again—until there were nine such groups! The "Jumbo Weekend" allowed them to come together again at least twice each year for a time of fellowship, sharing, and "reporting in."

Some eighty-eight persons joined us in the highlands above Zurich. They were of all ages and occupations, with one thing in common: they didn't speak English! As I sat through the times together, as they spoke and sang in Swiss-German, I became aware of several things.

First, I became aware of a level of communication which transcends mere words. I knew what they were saying even though I did not understand their words!

Second, I became aware of something even more astonishing: that what they were doing in their groups and on their retreats was exactly what we are doing in renewal in America! And, the same was true when I visited Paris, Geneva, Amsterdam, and Frankfurt! All alike, and with no comparison of notes either!

Reports filtering in from the Orient, Africa,

and South America indicate that such is true there, also.

What does it all say? Well, the echo I heard on the "Jumbo Weekend" in the Swiss Alps was: "God is up to something in his world today!"

It has to do with the laity, twice-born people who want to know more about their Lord and who want to share their reports of his activity in their lives.

It has to do with Bible study, prayer, fellowship, and witness. The fact that it is cropping up all around the world, and the fact that everywhere it looks alike, tells me that there is a design to it. I believe it is a new awakening.

Call it "renewal" or "revival" or whatever; God is up to something!

Renewal Reminder: *Remind me, O Lord, that you are up to something big **every** day. Amen.*

NOTES:

5. What to Do with "Staleness"

That is why I now remind you to stir into flame the gift of God which is within you through the laying on of my hands. For the spirit that God gave us is no craven spirit, but one to inspire strength, love, and self-discipline (2 Tim. 1:6–7, NEB).

All of us go through periods of staleness in our Christian lives, periods when our faith becomes a dull habit instead of an acute fever. In a time like that our first impulse is to counterfeit the absent glow with artifical expression and words. But, masking it does not cure it! Leighton Ford offers some practical advice in *The Christian Persuader* (New York: Harper and Row, 1966) on how to deal with it.

1. *I should acknowledge it to God and myself.* There is no use playing "let's pretend" with the searcher of hearts. If I am stale, he already knows it. If I am going through the old motions without the old power, I must admit it—much activity, little fruit.

2. *I should take time for spiritual inventory*—a half day or so alone with God and my Bible—allowing him to search my heart through his Word, to point out any area or act or attitude of disobedience, of unwillingness to be a servant for Jesus' sake. When the sin is discovered, the remedy is confession, cleansing, and a new commitment.

3. *I shall probably find genuine help* in the fellowship of a Christian friend, or group of believers. When there is a fellowship of openness, prayer, and concern, committed people can begin to be honest with one another and discover the dimension of apostolic fellowship.

4. *I may discover that my rut is largely a result of fatigue or monotony.* Someone has said that no man can be a philosopher when he has a toothache, and while a saint may sometimes get tired, it's very difficult to be tired and to feel saintly!

Renewal Reminder: *Remind me, O Lord, not to stall when I'm stale. Amen.*

NOTES:

6. Wouldn't It Be's????

*I am not writing thus to shame you, but
to bring you to reason; for you are my
dear children (1 Cor. 4:14, NEB).*

Have you ever stumbled into a swarm of
bees? To say the least, it is a stinging sensa-
tion! I periodically find myself accident-prone
in this direction. It happens to me occasionally, at seasons of contemplation—and I
stumble into that same swarm of bees—a
peculiar variety of bees that seem to bother
ministers more than anyone else. They are
called "Wouldn't It Be's."

Such is my present mental state, and the
"Wouldn't It Be's" are veritably stinging my
conscious thinking. Listen to them, as they
busily buzz my brain with thoughts of hope:

Wouldn't it be wonderful if we could find some

adequate means of expression to tell
our friends how much we really love
them!

Wouldn't it be a relief if we could "undo" the
actions on our part which so deeply
hurt other people . . . or, at least, if
everyone would prepare against such
future regrets by living out James 1:19.
"Beloved brethren, let every man be
swift to hear, slow to speak, slow to
wrath."

Wouldn't it be thrilling if all of us would come
alive at church and develop a disci-
plined practice of surrounding strang-
ers and new members with love and
attention.

Wouldn't it be exciting to fill our hallowed halls
with smiles each Sunday.

Wouldn't it be gratifying if everyone would
beware of half-truths and partial in-
formation, develop the grace of understanding, and always impute the finest
intentions upon others until we check
the real source of a misunderstanding
or problem.

Wouldn't it be blessed if people everywhere
could share in the love, the accomplishments, and the future destiny
of our church.

Wouldn't it be glorious if our hearts could be
gripped with the reality of the fact that
we are only limited by the measure of
our unavailability to the resplendent

27

fullness of Christ. "For in him dwelleth all the fulness of the Godhead bodily. And ye are complete in him" (Col. 2:9–10).

Wouldn't it be joyous if nursery workers were remembered, deacons were complimented, and attenders were appreciated, if all youngsters were encouraged and all oldsters were honored, and hundreds of our unheralded workers could be inundated with gratitude from those of us they help!

Wouldn't it be amazing if anybody did anything about what I've written!

Renewal Reminder: *Remind me, O Lord, to be something to someone today, rather than to try to be everything to everyone. Amen.*

NOTES:

7. Excess Baggage

*In all this, remember how critical the
moment is. It is time for you to wake out
of sleep, for deliverance is nearer to us
now than it was when first we believed. It
is far on in the night; day is near. Let us
therefore throw off the deeds of darkness
and put on our armour as soldiers of the
light (Rom. 13:11–12, NEB).*

If ever the church of Jesus Christ on earth
needed to travel fast and light, it is now. Far
too long we have been preoccupied with
good, but other-than-assigned tasks, and it is
telling (as never before) in so many areas.
Perhaps it is time to jettison some of our ex-
cess baggage. Like some of our

Beliefs.—The late Bishop Pike once said we
need "more belief and fewer beliefs." While I
do not agree with the particular beliefs he had
in mind, the principle is nonetheless valid.
Here I have reference to those treasured but
extra-biblical and peripheral beliefs that are
inconsequential to the salvation of souls and
the dignifying of human life.

Heritage.—I am always wary (and sometimes weary) when the church glories in its

past—to the exclusion of its future. Constant remembrance of the past is always potentially dangerous, for it saps a church's imagination for creative visions of the future and occupies the mind with idealized versions of the past! In light of the future, the past is a luxury we cannot presently afford.

Exclusivism.—While there are real and valid differences among the various branches of the church of Christ, differences which must not be ignored or even minimized, it seems to me that the formidable problems we all face are forcing us together. There is more than enough for all of us to do; indeed, more than all of us can do. Let's keep our boundary markers, but let's tear down the fences!

Ignorance.—The day is past and forever gone when we can expect to advance numerically and spiritually with uniformed troops. The life of witness today demands an informed church—biblically, theologically, and spiritually. The reading fare of the church must include, but go beyond, the reading (and mispronouncing) of missionarys' names and the merely inspirational. Depth and breadth of reading precede length and height of advance!

Open the hatch!

Renewal Reminder: *Remind me, O Lord, to keep the hatch open today. Amen.*

NOTES:

8. Days of High Visibility

"O God, thou art my God, I seek thee early with a heart that thirsts for thee and a body wasted with longing for thee" (Ps. 63:1, NEB).

Once, while reading among the many writings of Rufus Jones, I came upon one of his choice expressions—and he had many—that registered itself as a permanent guest in the memory room of my mind. Jones spoke of

"Days of High Visibility" in the spiritual life.

And, there are such days—days when the presence is real, the leadership evident, the way made plain, and the results rewarding. As I have reflected back over such days, in contrast to those many other "days of heavy overcast," in an effort to assess the manifest difference, I have found certain ingredients always present. While it is true that no amount of induced labor can ever produce such a day, there are certain elements inevitably evident.

First, they were days which were *prefaced with careful prayer*. Prayer that was not the usual list of complaints and requests, but rather that which sought and found communion with God. It was always prayer that scoured the soul for secret sin and where confident confession was made. It was prayer that confessed specific inadequacies and the lacking of divine desires. It was prayer that scanned the day ahead for possible occasions for God which sought sensitivity to it. It was prayer that enjoyed God, prayer that found itself no longer watching the clock, but, with time suspended, waiting on him.

Secondly, they were days which were *begun with the Bible*. It was not Bible study, for that is something vastly different. Rather, it was "communion reading." Invariably it was Bible reading prefaced by a verse I often quote or read before such reading to distinguish between devotion and study in my own mind:

"O God, my heart is ready" (Ps. 108:1, TLB). And, on these days of high visibility there has always been an awareness that the verses into which I ventured were *for me* that day. Inescapably so! The Word, then, becomes the quick and powerful two-edged sword discerning the intents of my woeful and wayward heart. It wounds it, breaks it, and then graciously heals it.

They are days when I know I have *companied* with him.

Others do, too. And, isn't that what it's all about?

Renewal Reminder: *Remind me, O Lord, that today might be a day of high visibility. Amen.*

NOTES:

9. Plan A—Plan B

And it is he who will supply all your needs from his riches in glory, because of what Christ Jesus has done for us (Phil. 4:19, TLB).

In trying to explain the reason for his coming, Jesus once said that an integral part of it was "that your joy might be full" (John 15:11).

A part of the joy which is our legacy from him is that which stems from our ability to trust him.

What a joy, what a delight it is to know things are never out of control! Never! The Creator has not relinquished his control of the universe nor removed his hand from the affairs of men. What confidence that creates in our hearts in every circumstance of life!

It is not to say that everything always goes our way or is what we might want. But it is to say that he is in control of every situation and will bring it to our good and his glory. One of the truly great promises of the Word is Romans 8:28. It says: "We know that in all things God works for good" (TEV), or, as J. B. Phillips translates it: "Moreover we know that to those who love God, who are called according to his plan, everything that happens fits into a pattern for good."

Linger long in the sunlight of that! Things

are never out of control! God is never at a loss as to what to do! We never destroy his "Plan A" but that God has a "Plan B!"

And, just now God is at work in your best interest. This is the joy of trust!

Renewal Reminder: *Remind me, O Lord, to simmer down; you really are able to handle today. Amen.*

NOTES:

10. Coming to the Pulpit

*For the preaching of the cross is to them
that perish foolishness; but unto us which
are saved it is the power of God (1 Cor.
1:18).*

I don't know when it first dawned on me,
but it did—and it is there yet: that attitude has
as much to do with coming to the pulpit as
does preparation, content, or delivery. Once
having recognized it, however, I have
gathered about me certain statements which
help to shape the attitude. And, since they are
behind-the-scenes guests every Sunday, let
me introduce them to you.

William Barclay. The Glasgow biblical
scholar starts my list with: "Every preacher
must try to give his people three things. He
must give them something to feel. He must
give them something to remember. He must
give them something to do."

Rufus Jones. In his inimitable way, Rufus
Jones says: "A minister ought to be to all of us
in our religious strivings what the artist is to
those who are eager for beauty, or what the
musician is to those who love music."

Elton Trueblood. Being both professor and
preacher, Elton Trueblood says: "The difference between a lecture and a sermon is that a
lecture has a subject, but a sermon has an

object."

John Claypool. This Baptist pastor once introduced a sermon with: "See me this morning as your burdened and broken brother, limping back into the family circle to tell you something of what I learned out there in the darkness."

The Bible. In Job 4:4, Eliphaz the Temanite spoke words to Job which ought to be coveted by every preacher. Moffatt translates it as: "Your words have kept men on their feet."

Soren Kierkegaard. While it was said about rather than by Kierkegaard, and of his writing rather than his preaching, it nonetheless constitutes a pulpit goal: "Kierkegaard conceived it his function as a writer to strip men of their disguises, to compel them to see evasions for what they are, to label blind alleys, to cut off men's retreats, to tear down the niggardly roofs they continue to build over their precious sundials, to isolate men from the crowd, to enforce self-examination, and to bring them solitary and alone before the Eternal. Here he left them."

Renewal Reminder: *Remind me, O Lord, that whether my pulpit is at the front of a church building or an office desk or a kitchen sink, you have called me to approach it in your Spirit and power. Amen.*

11. Is It OK to Fail at Your House?

For if they fall, the one will lift up his fellow: but woe to him that is alone when he falleth; for he hath not another to help him up. Again, if two lie together, then they have heat: but how can one be warm alone? (Eccl. 4:10–11).

It seems to me that the home ought to be one place where it is OK to fail. Take for instance a child who fails at school or in sports or in a relationship with another child. How should a parent respond? With anger? But, then, the child is angry with himself. With chiding? Saying "you're a failure" to a child who already knows it is little help!

How, then, are we to respond? First, be careful to distinguish between "being a failure" and "not coming up to your expectations." There is a difference in the two! Not coming up to your expectations may not be failure on the child's part, but on the parent's wrongly set goals. But, if it is failure, respond by helping. That may mean helping her with her homework or him with his passing the ball. It may mean encouraging, like the boy who was a failure at baseball until Dad went to see him play. Sometimes failure is really an appeal! It may mean accepting it, too. "Buster" may be a violinist rather than a fullback; and that means helping him to accept it, too, by being just as proud of his Mozart as his tackling.

Adults ought to be able to fail at home, too. Many a husband is driven beyond both his capacity and/or desire by a wife more in need of a symbol than a companion. And, when he fails, the response is often only added grief: a broken marriage instead of a made man! Likewise, many wives fail—at homework because they are born secretaries being jailed by men of adequate assets but antiquated attitudes—or at being a secretary because they are housewives by birth, being pushed outside the house in order to (ironically) make money to buy things "for the house!" How do we respond when our mates fail? How should we respond? By the same techniques: by helping and encouraging, and sometimes accepting it!

Together, Christ, the church, and Christians are in the business of helping others to become what God intended, not what we expect or anticipate. The home and the church are both called to be places of becoming. Let them, then, become becoming places!

Renewal Reminder: *Remind me, O Lord, of my own need to become and to help others, too. Amen.*

NOTES:

12. When the Earth Is Shaken, Dead Wood Falls

He said to them, "When, therefore, a teacher of the law has become a learner in the kingdom of Heaven, he is like a householder who can produce from his store both the new and old" (Matt. 13:52, NEB).

Progress is not always prized; in some churches it is despised! The earthshaking power of a vital church is quite a shock for the brittle spines of those at ease in Zion.

You see, when the earth is shaken, dead wood falls.

In a church, that dead wood is often represented by old traditions, old methods, and old practices that have become pillars of comfort for those who like things-as-they-are.

Like the old man said, "I have seen a thousand changes in this church during my twenty years as a member here, and I have been 'agin' every one of them." How human it is to be so distracted by the crash of outmoded methods that we fail to recognize the excellency of new accomplishments. When the old is felled, the whole forest echoes with its fall, but a hundred acorns are sown in silence by an unnoticed breeze.

Thank God for churches open and receptive

to each new day!

Yet, the art of progress is to preserve order amid change. We must balance our aspiration for progress with an ardor for orderliness. Grow on, oh, church, but let it be done decently and in order. The Holy Spirit will not work in confusion, yet progress must prevail. As Spurgeon said, "Every generation needs regeneration. Having adequately prepared, by all means, let the people come."

> I suppose I've passed it a hundred times,
> But I always stop a minute.
> And look at the house, the tragic house,
> The house with nobody in it.

Renewal Reminder: *Remind me, O Lord, to be a part of today and tomorrow, not yesterday. Amen.*

NOTES:

13. An Antireligious Age?

And when he is come, he will reprove the world of sin, and of righteousness, and of judgment (John 16:8).

We've been sold a bill of goods about religion. That's for sure!

It has to do with the unexamined premise that we are living in an antireligious era. To be sure, there is some evidence to indicate it. It's a fact that church attendance in America has been dropping 1 percent per year for over a decade now. It is down now to only 40 percent attending church. And, as we have redoubled our efforts in evangelizing the world and updated the church—without effect—we are slowly losing both our voice and our nerve. We are now telling ourselves that they won't listen anymore: We are living in an antireligious age.

Don't you believe it!

When I served as pastor in Annapolis, Maryland, Ralph Neighbour was visiting with us at Heritage Church. While there, he ventured down the street from his hotel to a bookstore where he met a sales representative. Ralph asked him about the hottest selling thing in books. His answer, he said, was a nationwide bestselling item. Care to guess? Astrology books!

No, we are not antireligious. Maybe antichurch, but certainly not antireligious. God simply made us otherwise. We can no more be antireligious than we can be antibreathing!

A few years ago I was in Paris studying this same phenomenon where attendance is down to about 20 percent of the members, not merely the population.

Jacques Blocher, a leader of evangelical Baptists and a seminary professor, told me how he had started a "dial-a-sermon" telephone effort. Over there the post office controls the telephone and one pays per call.

Even though the officials discouraged him ("We live in an antireligious age"), especially at the point of thinking that "pagan Parisians" would pay for a sermon, he went ahead. At the end of one week, the calls had so jammed the switchboard that they had to add another line. By the end of the month they had added nine lines: 40,000 calls per month! His answer to my question—Why?—was: "People may be antichurch at present, but they are not antireligious."

It is true that we are obviously living in an era when the church is being rejected. But that's a different thing altogether than saying that people are antireligious. They cannot be—by design. God's design. Consequently, they are being fed at other tables: astrology, Oriental religions, and the like.

Renewal has this problem as its focus. On one hand, we see the church in need of renewal. On the other hand, we see the church in need of realizing that our voice is still in vogue. I personally believe that a mobilized laity is the answer to both the renewal of the church as well as the evangelization of the world.

Renewal Reminder: *Remind me, O Lord, to assume that you are at work around me and in me. Amen.*

NOTES:

14. Easter: Wrong Word— Right Time

Late that Sunday evening, when the disciples were together behind locked doors, for fear of the Jews, Jesus came and stood among them. "Peace be with you!" he said, and then showed them his hands and his side. So when the disciples saw the Lord, they were filled with joy. Jesus repeated, "Peace be with you!", and said, "As the Father sent me, so I send you" (John 20:19–21, NEB).

The word *Easter* is the "English-ization" of the name of the pagan love goddess Astarte. The sensuous festivals of this fertility religion were held annually in the spring of the year. As unconverted pagans became paganized converts, the word was such a familiar part of their vocabularies and the season was such a part of their lives that they simply carried over the name to the resurrection celebration which also occurred at the same time of the year! "Easter" is used only once in the King James Version (Acts 12:4), but it is a mistranslation of the word *pasche* which means Passover.

It is the wrong word, but the right time!

But little does it matter, really! The crucial matter is that we mark well the event: the bodily resurrection of our Lord from the tomb.

And, far more important than the "that" of it is the "why" of it.

He arose that he might ever be in the midst and in the hearts of his own.

He arose to break the power of sin and death over us and give us hope and life eternal.

He arose to encounter men like us in our lives to add dimensions of living previously unknown.

He arose to tell us to tell others that he arose!

Each Easter, the reactions of the pulpits will widely vary regarding the resurrection. Some deny it; others demythologize it; some defend it.

Let's declare it!

Renewal Reminder: *Remind me, O Lord, that you live today. Amen.*

NOTES:

15.   Spring Has Sprung!

We were called God's children, and such we are; and the reason why the godless world does not recognize us is that it has not known him. Here and now, dear friends, we are God's children; what we shall be has not yet been disclosed, but we know that when it is disclosed we shall be like him, because we shall see him as he is. Everyone who has this hope before him purifies himself, as Christ is pure (1 John 3:1–3, NEB).

For several days now we have enjoyed the warm days of sunshine which suggests that spring is finally here. Oh, to be sure, we yet will face an intermittent, uninvited cool breeze. Nevertheless, we know the days just ahead will be joyous days of spring. Hallelujah!

To me, there is no time quite as exciting as the spring of each year. Take a good look at the bright, radiant springtime. It is God's smile. Wailing storms and sobbing rains have fallen dead at the feet of spring, and the tree branches, at this moment, are telegraphs sending the news ahead, "Spring has come! Spring has come!"

Do you realize the mercy of the Lord in the dominant color of springtime? He might have covered the earth with a dull brown, depressing us with melancholy. Or, he might have covered the earth with crimson red, wearying the eye with its strange blaze. But no! He covers the earth with the dominant color which is most appropriate for a long while—a gentle, living green! Against that dominant green, the beauty of all God's colors are a dazzling display of his goodness to men.

Yes, and springtime always suggests to me the resurrection glory awaiting us in heaven. If this world, blasted with sin and swept with storms, is still so beautiful—which is but the corpse of a dead paradise—the charred hulk of a giant vessel which floundered in the dawn of life, and has ever since been beating on the rocks—I say, if this world, notwithstanding all the curse of sin, is so beautiful, what will it be like in the heavenly paradise to which we go!

Oh, that will be the day, when the final spring has come!

Renewal Reminder: *Remind me, O Lord, to live in the sunshine. Amen.*

16. Jesus Does All Things Well—As We Ask!

But my God shall supply all your need according to his riches in glory by Christ Jesus (Phil. 4:19).

Recently, I attended a gathering of the men in our church. We ate supper together, then spent an hour together in a happy and stimulating exchange of Christian experience. However, just as it was time to leave, I realized that one of the men had seemed uneasy in my presence all evening. It had puzzled me and worried me, because I was acutely aware of our difference in opinion about a recent matter. I walked away into a night of gloom. Like an unwanted guest on a vacation, the presence of that worry-thought in my mind began to squelch all my joy. It matters to me what my men think—and my thoughts about one man were about to sour the sweet interchange I had experienced with all the others.

Suddenly, I thought of Christ, and my mental equilibrium returned. "Lord Jesus," I prayed, "I am going to put my preaching into practice, and trust you for help in this problem. I am not going to worry over that which is hardly a challenge to you. I acknowledge and appropriate your presence, in the faith you will live in my life to love that man to thyself and, thus, unto me."

With the hilarious joy of knowing my problem was his, I entered my car and drove off singing.

On the way between the church door and my car he made the difference, and my night was saved from the wiles of a devil who was about to snatch victory away.

In countless ways, Christ can prove sufficient for every need if we will enter a state of constantly conscious dependence upon him.

Already, I have the joy of faith's assurance in the competence of Christ. Yesterday, I felt a melting, magical empathy, between that man and myself. Given time, Christ will make us inseparable companions.

Jesus does all things well—as we ask!

Do you release every problem to him?

Renewal Reminder: *Remind me, O Lord, to release today and myself to you. Amen.*

NOTES:

17. Given to Hospitality

The night is far spent, the day is at hand: let us therefore cast off the works of darkness, and let us put on the armour of light (Rom. 13:12).

The most beautiful thing in the house of God should be the grace of hospitality displayed by its worshipers. Stained windows, golden candlesticks, and plush carpets will never impress the friend or stranger who steps across the threshold as will the warmth of our greeting, the informality of our reception, and the reiteration of our warmest welcome by grasp and by look and by a thousand almost insignificant attentions.

Have you ever attended a church and felt you were an uninvited guest? A stranger, you stand in the vestibule for a while, then make a pilgrimage down the long aisle. No place of seating opens until, flushed and embarrassed, you start back again. Then, coming to some half-filled pew, with an apologetic air you enter it, while the immovable occupant seated by the aisle glares at you with a look which seems to say, "Well, if I must, I must." So you sit there as uncomfortable as a centipede with athlete's foot!

Since I have never seen a black flower, I conclude that God intended to plant brightness along our paths. It is certainly so in our greeting of those who come to God's house, for each of us should learn to "shew himself friendly" (Prov. 18:24).

It's an actual fact that a very general opinion of the non-Christian world is that church people are as stuck-up as a billboard. They received their impression of us while visiting our Sunday morning worship services, in which we act like it's our sacred duty to be snooty. We stick our noses so high in the air that we have developed a double chin on the back of our neck. We are so ritzy we wear riding habits to pitch horseshoes!

But let the bells toll twelve, and worshipers dismissed, the Christians are suddenly transformed to the most warmhearted people on earth.

Let not the church be known as a stately and reticent friend, hard to get at!

Rather, let us be as approachable as a country mansion on a summer day when all the doors and windows are wide open.

Renewal Reminder: *Remind me, O Lord, to be as a host, not a guest, in your world. Amen.*

NOTES:

18. But Beware the Lightning!

Wilt thou not revive us again: that thy people may rejoice in thee? (Ps. 85:6).

The glory clouds fill our sky! Hallelujah! The weather vane points toward a climate of awakening. Heavenly breezes are refreshing us, sprinkled blessings are exciting us, and the glory clouds hover over the church.

Thank God for those clouds, and take hope! They hover there as a visible evidence that God has heard our prayers. Showers of blessings will come!

However, this is the time to beware!

Lightning never strikes out of a clear sky.

The same clouds that provide the shower,

55

also foster an occasional thunderbolt! The church is being refreshed by the showers, but Christian fellowship can be shattered by the thunderbolt!

Like white lightning, the devil's thunderbolt can strike in a flash and set a church ablaze with hot debate, sizzling frictions, and burning conflict.

Better install some lightning rods! Satan will strike through those clouds. Lightning is attracted by a moving target—especially a church on the move!

Nevertheless, praise God for glory clouds.

Lightning never falls out of a blue sky; but neither will showers of blessing—and a downpour is what we need!

"Mercy drops round us are falling, But for the showers we plead."

Renewal Reminder: *Remind me, O Lord, that you are the giver of the rain and the sun. Amen.*

NOTES:

19. Spiritual Remedies

Blessed be the God and Father of our Lord Jesus Christ, who hath blessed us with all spiritual blessings in heavenly places in Christ (Eph. 1:3).

I was blessed at a recent denominational pastor's conference.

The speakers diagnosed our illnesses with the penetrating accuracy of a physician. All our maladies were clearly exposed—as they should be—that we may eradicate every sickness in the body!

However, what rattled my spiritual stethoscope were the remedies those good doctors suggested!

Am I in error to suggest the one great remedy was entirely overlooked? Is not our real sickness within the individual Christian?

Assuredly, the complex worlds of modern man require skillful ministry if our witness is to penetrate the cold fog of their sophisticated isolation. Nevertheless, the inner dynamic and convicting power for such penetration must come from within me!

The glaring deficiency in the American pulpit is the gross neglect of preaching on the inward spiritual renewal of the individual Christian.

Victory is ours when the indwelling Christ lives out his life in us. Is this not the remedy for anemic Christianity? I believe it is! My prognosis is a renewal of emphasis upon the ministry of the Holy Spirit in the inward man—Christ diffused through real human life that is indwelt by him. Label the emphasis what you will—deeper life, the exchanged life, the abundant life, the spirit-filled life, the abiding life—we need a refreshing biblical emphasis upon the message of the indwelling Christ, by whatever term it may be described.

Our world will meet its Savior as we learn to allow him the expression of himself through us.

Renewal Reminder: *Remind me, O Lord, that I am the most "me" when you are "you" in me. Amen.*

NOTES:

20. Did You See that Picture?

Say not ye, There are yet four months, and then cometh harvest? behold, I say unto you. Lift up your eyes, and look on the fields; for they are white already to harvest (John 4:35).

I was startled by a recent newspaper war picture. The photograph captured the grimace of pain on the face of a squatting peasant. Lying beside him, sprawled on her back, was the lifeless body of his wife. Her feet were bare, her head rested in her broadbrimmed Oriental sun hat, her arms were spread wide, and her mouth hung open and breathless. Beside the mother lay the son, his shirt ripped open by bullets and his body bloody with gaping wounds. Both mother and child were innocent victims of the cross fire of guns.

Most of us scarcely noticed that picture, far less remembered it two seconds later. Two souls were swept out of life into eternity; a photographer shared their tragedy with the world; but who cared? A lonely, grief-stricken father still weeps in the night, but not one of us can identify with his plight.

You see, the disaster occurred too far away, and somehow the death of a peasant is different. Their feet were bare and dirty. Their features were lean and gaunt. Their clothes were old and shabby. Not much was lost in their passing. Even neighbors will scarcely care. Certainly, we shall not feel concern.

But they say there was a time when America cared—just because God cares! A time when the world saw America as a knight in shining armor, dashing to the rescue of the oppressed and plundered. Now, the American image is a fat-jawed, cigar-smoking opportunist, haughty, and hated by the world.

We've no time now for the problems of other worlds. We are busy with important things. There is television to view, and snacks to eat, and friends to phone, and games to watch, and trips to take, and golf to play, and parties to hold, and hair to be fixed, and socials to attend, and cocktails to drink, and gossip to share, and money to spend, and bingo to win, and movies to see, and vacations to enjoy, and friends to entertain, and bull to shoot, and lawns to mow, and loafing to do, and jokes to tell, and magazines to read,

and cakes to bake . . .
    . . . while our world goes on to hell!

Renewal Reminder: *Remind me, O Lord, to be about your work today. Amen.*

NOTES:

21. About Hardship!

But we have this treasure in earthen ves-
sels, that the excellency of the power may
be of God, and not of us. We are troubled
on every side, yet not distressed; we are
perplexed, but not in despair; Persecuted,
but not forsaken; cast down, but not de-
stroyed; Always bearing about in the body
the dying of the Lord Jesus, that the life
also of Jesus might be made manifest in
our body (2 Cor. 4:7–10).

Someone asked, "Why is life so difficult for a Christian? Doesn't God love us?"

A part of the answer is that the hardship of life should best be considered the very evidence of God's love. Surely, if God really loves us, he will not be content with us as we are. His love must, in the nature of things, be impeded and repelled by our imperfect character. Just because God loves us he will make us lovable, which indeed is our highest good. C. S. Lewis calls it our "intolerable compliment."

Speakman is correct in rebelling against the song which says: "Somebody up there likes me . . ."

Nobody up there likes you. Somebody up there loves you. That song sounds too nice and cozy and easy and comforting! Its lyrics are a full page ad for thin, soupy, watered-down sentimentalism which so many people vaguely believe is the Christian faith.

God doesn't just like us, he loves us. Because God loves us some tension will always exist as a result of his enmity against all that is wrong in us and his pull toward all that is best for us unto perfect holiness.

Would our world be better without hardship? "Better for what?" asks Lofton Hudson. If we are so childish as to think the goal of life is comfort, security, and pleasure, then the hardships of life will never make sense. If, on the other hand, the goal of life is growing great people, surely it is well to live in such a world of challenge.

In our weakness his strength is made perfect!

Renewal Reminder: *Remind me, O Lord, that you alone are my strength and my salvation. Amen.*

NOTES:

22. Enthusiasm Is the Genius of Sincerity

Rejoice evermore (1 Thess. 5:16).

A father was bewildered. His teenage daughter was impatient to leave for a concert which featured a popular singing group. "I just don't understand it," he said to her. "Why do you bother to go? You are all screaming so, you don't hear them anyway." "My word, Daddy," she said, "you don't go to hear them. You go to scream! If you want to hear them, you buy their record!"

Of course! It's a matter of enthusiasm!

The idea is to have a cause, a hero; someone or something to shout about—to get excited about.

Well, come on into the Kingdom. Out in God's country we walk on shouting ground! Our enthusiasm is inexhaustible, sparked by experiences with a cosmically-enthroned God.

Why, the very word itself is a Christian word. Enthusiasm is derived from the Greek word *entheos* which means "God in you" or "full of God." A Christian is enthusiastic, for his inner being pulsates with the wondrous life of the indwelling God!

I tell you, nothing is as self-contradictory as a sourpuss saint!

Yet, you find them—occasionally.

I chatted with one just recently. He was as stimulating as a hearse and as exciting as a graveyard on a wet Sunday. He had a disposition of an untipped waiter; the kind of guy who stays as sore as a porcupine with ingrown quills. He's always blowing out the light to see how dark it is.

Of course, this person was a Baptist preacher—but a variety of this breed infects almost every church.

Let there be no room for them with us! Our cause deserves enthusiastic members who will produce a singing church, a growing church, a united church, a loving church, a sacrificial church, and an evangelistic church!

If it were as easy to arouse enthusiasm as it is discouragement, just think what could be accomplished!

Renewal Reminder: *Remind me, O Lord, that I don't have to act like a Christian; I just need to be one. Amen.*

NOTES:

23. Cross-bearing

Then said Jesus unto his disciples, If any man will come after me, let him deny himself, and take up his cross, and follow me (Matt. 16:24).

What an awesome humiliation, to be forced to bear one's own cross to the place of execution! But, half-dead from his brutal scourging, weakened from the loss of blood and lack of food and sleep, Jesus sagged to his knees while two guards hooked the heavy cross over his shoulders. At the crack of a whip across his back, Christ lifted his burden and staggered forward down the dolorous way. His robe was stiff with caked blood from his scourgings. His hair was matted with blood drawn from a crown of thorns which still hung on his brow. Half-stumbling and half-lurching forward he moved along, becoming increasingly aware of added pain as the heavy beam began biting deep into his shoulder, piercing deeper each time it bounced along behind him. He buckled under its load. He locked his jaws, but groaned inwardly, his nerves stinging intensely as if they were red-hot wires strung through his body. His muscles stretched in agonizing pain.

A hundred yards seemed like a hundred miles, the pain growing more intense. His breath came in suffocating gasps now, for the intensive heat of the Judean sun made even the air around him almost stifling. Soon the ground gave way under his feet, casting him headfirst, his face crashing into the rocky road, scraping and gashing his nose, cheeks, and brow. The heavy beam raked the skin from his back. One soldier walked over and kicked him; another lashed out with a whip; but somehow he staggered forward again. By now his mind was only half-lucid, stunned with the throbbing thistles of pain. Blood kept filling his eyes, but occasionally he could discern faces through the red film; gaunt faces which gaped with wild enjoyment at his spectacle. They seemed a wide sea of faces like wild animals with beady eyes taunting him, cursing, screaming, spitting, and throwing rocks and refuse at his shame. Further exertion caused more blood to ooze from his thorn-pierced brow, filling his eyes. Blinded, he lost all sense of direction, and the soldiers howled with laughter, prodding him as he groped from one direction to another.

Yes, dear Christian, I know what you are thinking! The cross we bear seems so severe at times, but so was his!

Renewal Reminder: *Remind me, O Lord, not to forget my cross as I go forth today. Amen.*

NOTES:

24. The Magic of a Moment

And let us consider one another to provoke unto love and to good works: Not forsaking the assembling of ourselves together, as the manner of some is; but exhorting one another: and so much the more, as ye see the day approaching (Heb. 10:24–25).

There is a whine of complaint issuing from the church and echoing across our nation. Christian leaders are decrying the decreased attendance in Sunday and Wednesday night services. People are spending less and less time at church. For the majority, their presence in God's house is now almost limited to one hour on Sunday morning.

The complaint is accurate, but I am weary of hearing it!

Why whine? This issue is desperate! Our troops are near desertion and all some come up with is a whimper! At least we still have that one hour! Sanctify this sixty minutes, dear churches. God doesn't sleep late on Sunday. He takes morning appointments. Schedule him in!

I tell you, one hour can be more than adequate time for God! He doesn't even need an hour; just a moment! Using just the refrain of a song, or the turn of a sentence, God can confront us in a moment and the impression lingers for a lifetime. Oh, the magic of a moment when God is in it! In the twinkle of an eye, God comes smashing through our selfishness for our moment of truth. A man is never quite the same after a visit from God!

Give Sunday's saints just a few seconds with God. Allow them an audience with him. Let them relish just one moment of such spiritual ecstasy in every worship hour and I dare say our auditoriums would not contain the crowds!

I leave you with one of the most profound remarks of our day, by Dr. Kinlow of Asbury College: "Give me one Divine moment when God acts and I say that moment is far superior to all the human efforts of man throughout the centuries."

Meet this Sunday, not to whine, but to worship!

Renewal Reminder: *Remind me, O Lord, to anticipate a moment today. Amen.*

NOTES:

25. How You Look Is Important

But the Lord said unto Samuel, Look not on his countenance, or on the height of his stature: because I have refused him: for the Lord seeth not as man seeth; for man looketh on the outward appearance, but the Lord looketh on the heart (1 Sam. 16:7).

Sociologists, ethnologists, and psychologists jointly say that, apparently for reasons of personal security, all peoples "look down" on some other segment of the human race. While it is not a necessity, it seems to be a sociological and psychological inevitability.

Illustrations of it abound. The whites look down on the blacks almost everywhere. In the Southwest, where blacks are few, it is the Mexicans. Bostonians once looked down on the immigrants. The natives of the industrial North look down on the Southerners who have migrated there for employment. The DAR has the tendency to look down on later arrivals. And, it is not just an American phenomenon. In the Caribbean, purebloods look down on the mixed bloods. In India, Hindus look down on Muslims. Israelis look down on Arabs. And, on and on—universally so.

Who do you look down on?

Whoever it is, it is wrong! In fact, it is sin!

For the Christian, however, there are even more haunting, probing questions than merely, "Who do you look down on?" Questions like:

Who looks to you—for a word from God?

Who looks up to you—for an exemplification of Christ?

How grateful all of us ought to be that one day one looked down on us in mercy and caused us to look up and taught us to look out for one another, not down on.

Think about it!

Look into it!

Renewal Reminder: *Remind me, O Lord, to see as you see today. Amen.*

NOTES:

26. Psychoceramic Mail

(Crackpots!)

Go ye therefore, and teach all nations, baptizing them in the name of the Father, and of the Son, and of the Holy Ghost: Teaching them to observe all things whatsoever I have commanded you: and, lo, I am with you alway, even unto the end of the world (Matt. 28:19–20).

One of the results of serving a downtown church is that the pastor receives a steady stream of crank mail. It varies in subject matter, sometimes being a new revelation from God, sometimes the report of a vision, and sometimes the good Lord alone knows what it is about! The most common characteristic of them all is that they are usually unsigned—for which, after reading, I don't usually blame them!

Not long ago, I received what must be the latest from the Lord. The revelation arrived in a plain envelope, with no return address. It was postmarked from a nearby city and was addressed to me in what appeared to be feminine handwriting. Inside was a booklet—nothing more. After reading it, I am now able to relay to you "God's latest." Ready?

"The Great Commission has been revoked! Indeed, a greater commission has been given [although the booklet did not say what it was], so that now we are no longer to preach the gospel nor to baptize with water. Just what we are to do apparently hasn't been revealed yet, but perhaps the next installment will tell us. O yes, there is an address given so that we can send our offerings. I guess that's called "Revelations of the Installment Plan."

Aren't you glad we've been informed of this change in plans? Wouldn't it have been tragic had we gone on preaching and baptizing? I don't know how this is going to affect those who have been baptized lately for, you see, the booklet was undated and I don't know when this new plan went into effect. But, since we are not sure of just what we are to do until the next installment comes through, if all parties concerned do not mind, I think I'll just stick with the old Great Commission. Besides, I haven't completed it yet, anyway!

Renewal Reminder: *Remind me, O Lord, to be faithful today, not fancy. Amen.*

NOTES:

27. Hollywood Has Sown to the Wind

I said to myself, "Come, I will plunge into pleasures and enjoy myself"; but this too was emptiness. Of laughter I said, "It is madness!" (Eccl. 2:1, NEB).

Mr. Eric Johnson, speaking as president of the Motion Picture Association of America, asked one of the most shameless questions of our day. "Why, despite our unceasing efforts, does the film industry fail at times to have public confidence?" Then he had the unmitigated gall to suggest, "The public should take pride in the fact that we have amended our production code to keep up with the times and reflect our society." This statement was offered as the reason for the sadism, sex, and sensualism of the silver screen.

That statement is as sane as a lunatic's dream! The typical Hollywood sales pitch—those guys could pin badges on frankfurters and sell them as police dogs!

But you say that I, as a minister, am prejudiced. That's right! So allow me to share a documented answer from a qualified authority. In a speech to the National Board of Review, Bosley Crowther, motion picture critic of the *New York Times*, said: "I do not believe that the motion pictures of today, or any time for that matter, have in the majority of cases reflected life as it is actually lived. I doubt if you believe they have either. Last night I made a very careful check on the pictures which I have been seeing this year. There were close to 200 of them. I could not find more than four or five which I felt gave a true and accurate approximation of the segments of life which they pretended to represent. Literally speaking, therefore, I am convinced that Hollywood does not express America."

Next, allow me to quote another unbiased observer and add the final comment which perfectly expresses my thought on this subject. "Can anyone deny that movies are dirtier than ever? But they don't call it dirt. Why do we nod owlishly when they tell us that filth is merely a daring art form, that licentiousness is really social comment? Isn't it plain that the financially harassed movie industry is putting gobs of sex in darkened theaters in an effort to lure curious teenagers away from their TV sets?"

The headquarters of Hollywood is located in the box office. It's cash that counts, and it's sex that sells! So Hollywood has sown to the wind and our children will reap the whirlwind.

Renewal Reminder: *Remind me, O Lord, to sow to the Spirit today, not the wind. Amen.*

28.   The Crowing of the Cock

"I am the vine, and you the branches. He who dwells in me, as I dwell in him, bears much fruit; for apart from me you can do nothing" (John 15:5, NEB).

For three years, with the best of intentions, Peter tried to be a Christian. He displayed a marked personal determination and sincerity toward the Lord Jesus.

Just the night before Calvary, Peter said, "Lord, why cannot I follow thee now? I will lay down my life for thy sake" (John 13:37).

But the Lord didn't take Peter seriously. He placed little value on Peter's loyalty, love, and enthusiasm. Because Jesus knew Peter for all his sincerity, for all his service, and though willing to mobilize all his human resources on Christ's behalf, he did not have what it takes. Jesus said, "Before the cock crows you will have denied me three times" (John 13:38, NEB).

Jesus did not doubt Peter's sincere profession; he was unimpressed with Peter's ability to perform! You see, Peter was trying to accomplish the spiritually impossible. He was trying to be a Christian without Christ. He was attempting to run his Christian life on human resources.

The result was abject failure. In the course of events which followed, Peter was placed on trial. As the night drew to a close, and the moonlight was withdrawing slowly across the cobblestones, Peter began to follow afar off. Soon, he refused to suffer the cold of early morning and went over to warm himself by the enemies' fire. It was there that a little peasant girl challenged his discipleship. Three times Peter firmly denied his Lord. Then, suddenly, the early morning lull was broken with the shrill announcement of day by the crowing of a cock. Remembering the words of his Lord, he went out and wept bitterly.

Nevertheless, it is a wonderful moment in our spiritual experience when the cock crows. For the crowing of the cock is the herald of dawn. Yes, for most of us, it is only out of the bitter night of self-discovery that we turn to the Son of glory, for the bright new day that he alone can give. Then every horizon will beckon with golden prospect, as bright as the promises of God.

That decisive turn from self-effort gives Jesus the opportunity to be all that he is in you. It takes Christ to be a Christian. Only he can live it, and he will as you make your life available to all he wishes to be in terms of you.

Renewal Reminder: *Remind me, O Lord, to be available, just available. Amen.*

NOTES:

29. Give Dad a Double-Breasted Suit for Father's Day

But for your part, stand by the truths you have learned and are assured of. Remember from whom you learned them; remember that from early childhood you have been familiar with the sacred writings which have power to make you wise and lead you to salvation through faith in Christ Jesus (2 Tim. 3:14–15, NEB).

The fashion magazines all say that double-breasted suits are back in style! And that makes me happy! I am so glad because there are so many cherished memories about them for me—for, you see, my Dad wore one. It was a bold, blue pinstriped one with lapels at least a foot wide and cuffs that could fit over a barrel with room to spare! And how he loved to wear it!

Every Sunday morning he put it on and we walked together to church. We walked—and thereby hangs a tale (pleated, of course). When the war came, and with it the rationing of gas, all the available family resources were taken to feed, clothe, and house three growing boys. The only extra compensation for operating an automobile was his weekly tithe. What did he do? He sold the car, kept tithing, and we walked! And Dad walked in front in his double-breasted suit.

Yes, we walked. It was only a half mile or so. Through sunshine, snow, and rain we walked every Sunday, without fail. And Dad wore that double-breasted suit.

On Sunday afternoon he took it off and we all played at home together. You do remember those days when families were families, don't you?

Then, late Sunday evening, Dad would put it on again and we walked to Sunday night preaching. And every Sunday night, too! Sometimes we left folks sitting until we returned. Dad was kinda funny about that. He believed we boys needed Bible training.

Often through the week, in addition to the regular midweek prayer meeting, we would venture near and far to attend a revival. Baptist work in our area was young then, and we had to help make a crowd. And Dad always wore that double-breasted suit.

Yes, double-breasted suits are coming back. I could wish that double-breasted faith was coming back, too!

Like Dad's!

Renewal Reminder: *Remind me, O Lord, to live for the Father, today. Amen.*

30. Whose Side Are You Really On?

For it is by his grace you are saved, through trusting him; it is not your own doing. It is God's gift, not a reward for work done. There is nothing for anyone to boast of. For we are God's handiwork, created in Christ Jesus to devote ourselves to the good deeds for which God has designed us (Eph. 2:8–10, NEB).

The story is told of the contractor who built a church for an aggressive and growing church and then could not get them to pay for it. He decided to scare them into paying and rented a devil's suit, complete with horns, a tail, and a spear.

One Sunday night, as the preacher was inveighing against the congregation with hellfire and brimstone, the builder flipped off the lights and bounded down the aisle. Panic struck and people rushed for the doors. One spry old saint stumbled and fell right at his feet. The disguised builder loomed over her with spear in hand to scare the wits out of her. She struggled to her knees and in quivering voice said:

"O Mr. Devil, hear me please! I've baked more cakes, washed more dishes, taught more Sunday School classes, and made more visits than any other woman in this church. But don't be fooled—I've been on your side all the time!"

Could it be that some so-called church members have done all these things and more, and yet have been on his side all along?

We get on God's side only through being born again. Our works do not get us on God's side, ever, no matter how good or how many. Our fellowship with God is a gift not an achievement. Only as we yield the control of our lives to him do we receive that which cannot be bought or earned—the new birth.

Nor do we stay on God's side by our works. All of salvation is of and by grace as a gift. Our fellowship with him is always on the basis of his gracious love and mercy. We are saved and kept by grace and grace alone.

But, our works do evidence whose side we are on! The apostle Paul spoke of some in these words: "They profess that they know God; but in works, they deny him" (Titus 1:16).

Whose side are you on?

Renewal Reminder: *Remind me, O Lord, to be clear today about whose side I'm on, all day long. Amen.*

NOTES:

31. Divinity in Clay

The secret is this: Christ in you, the hope
of a glory to come (Col. 1:27, NEB).

The Christian life can be lived!

In that one measured sentence, I have stated the most startling discovery of my salvation. Oh, for years I questioned it. I still need to be constantly reminded of it. But I do, at least, believe it. The Christian life can be lived!

That's headline news in our day. For ours is the age of spiritual dropouts. The Baptists bow out, the Roman Catholics rust out, the Fundamentalists fall out, the Ecumenicals cop out, the students stalk out, the hippies hide out, our workers wear out, our crusade converts cut out, and our old soldiers of the cross just fade away!

However, I believe the one clear rally cry to renew our forces would be this glorious reaffirmation: The Christian life can be lived!

However, it must also be said that the Christian life cannot be lived by just everybody. Nor, just anybody. But only by the one great somebody, Jesus Christ, our Lord. That's the secret of a spiritual life. The Christian life can be lived, but only by Christ.

You must have the right one living it! Liberace is an accomplished pianist, but he would be a disaster as a tackle for the Green Bay Packers. "Hoss" Cartwright played the role of a cowboy to perfection, but he would have been less than graceful as a ballet dancer for the Metropolitan Opera Company! Opinion is down on the Christian life today; but there is nothing wrong with the Christian life if you have the right person living it.

The Christian life can be lived by Christ! It is exclusively his to live. He *designed* it to be lived. He *assigned* it to be lived. But only by himself.

That's why the Christian life is so difficult. You are forever trying to live it, in your own strength, when it can only be lived in dependence upon him. This is the sum and substance of the spiritual way of life. It is an exchanged life. You exchange your life for Christ's so that he might live his life in you.

"I am crucified with Christ: nevertheless I live; yet not I, but Christ liveth in me" (Gal. 2:20).

Renewal Reminder: *Remind me, O Lord, to let you live in me that I might live and radiate life. Amen.*

NOTES:

32. Human Relations Rule No. 1

"Always treat others as you would like them to treat you: that is the Law and the prophets" (Matt. 7:12, NEB).

CONFUCIUS (500 B.C.): What you don't want done to yourself, don't do to others.

BUDDHA (400 B.C.): Hurt not others with that which pains thyself.

ZOROASTER (400 B.C.): Do not do unto others all that which is not well for oneself.

PLATO (300 B.C.): May I do to others as I would that they should do unto me.

JUDAISM (Hillel, first century B.C.): What is hateful to yourself, don't do to your fellowman.

JESUS (first century): Do for others just what you want them to do for you (Luke 6:31, TEV).

SIKHISM (sixteenth century): Treat others as thou wouldst be treated thyself.

KANT (nineteenth century): So conduct yourself that you can wish that your actions might become universal law.

But, alas, as someone else concluded: We have not tried it and found it wanting; we have found it difficult and not tried it! After 2,500 years of encouragement, isn't it about time we. . . .

Renewal Reminder: *Remind me, O Lord, that no matter who said it, or how, it is still true and still works. Amen.*

NOTES:

33. The Danger of Spiritual Blur

And what of ourselves? With all these witnesses to faith around us like a cloud, we must throw off every encumbrance, every sin to which we cling, and run with resolution the race for which we are entered, our eyes fixed on Jesus, on whom faith depends from start to finish: Jesus who, for the sake of the joy that lay ahead of him, endured the cross, making light of its disgrace, and has taken his seat at the right hand of the throne of God (Heb. 12:1–2, NEB).

The picture of your Christian life, can be badly distorted when you fail to focus your eyes properly.

You see, Christians must always keep their eyes on Christ if everything else is to be seen in proper perspective.

His is a simple, irrefutable law of life. Without Christ as the central focus of interest, everything and everyone else will have the tendency to either loom too large or fade out of the picture.

Take your eyes off Christ:

> And faults and failures in the church can loom so large.
> The path ahead can seem so hopeless.
> The difficulties can seem so defeating.

The means at hand can seem so inadequate.

The circumstances involved can be so confusing.

Even our experience at church can be so uninspiring.

Yes, and the wounds we suffer appear so severe, unless we keep in view those nail-scarred hands!

Almost all of us have had the misfortune of failing to turn the film in our camera after taking a picture. Therefore upon receiving the print from the developer, we become the victims of a double exposure. What a blurred, unintelligible, mixed-up picture we get!

But the picture is always bright and clear when we keep our eyes on him!

Think on it!

Renewal Reminder: *Remind me, O Lord, to see you more clearly, love you more dearly, follow you more nearly, day by day. Amen.*

NOTES:

34. The Fine Art of Plowing Around the Stump

Let us then pursue the things that make
for peace and build up the common life
(Rom. 14:19, NEB).

I was reared in the piney woods country of deep East Texas. The tall, pine trees were breathtaking in their beauty, and we cherished them like forest treasures until the occasion when one had to be removed. It wasn't the cutting of the tree that was difficult, but the removing of that stump!

That's one thing we learned in East Texas—the art of stump removal!

Most of us know what it is to be stumped by a problem. Engaged in some noble project, we plow a straight row of progress until, suddenly, a stump impedes our path.

What is the proper course of action for a time like this? Well, there are several ways to remove a stump!

You can employ a bulldozer method and pound away at your problem until it is uprooted and removed. However, problems severe enough to stump us are usually stubborn and deep rooted. Their forced removal is a tedious process. It necessitates tearing away surrounding earth, digging down to cut away the roots, followed by endless pounding and jarring. One does not easily bulldoze through a tough problem.

I have seen men burn stumps away, but this depends on the nature of the wood and requires a deep-burning, well-tended fire. We would do well to learn this method. Never underestimate the effectiveness of a warm, deeply felt Christian love in dissolving problems.

Similarly, for certain kinds of stumps, we would do well to learn the method of the patient farmer. His method is one of the very best. I speak of "the fine art of plowing around the stump," as most problems will rot away if one gives them time.

Renewal Reminder: *Remind me, O Lord, to look to you for wisdom in dealing with my stumps. Amen.*

NOTES:

35. Browsing in My Sermon File

It is not to be thought that I have already achieved all this. I have not yet reached perfection, but I press on, hoping to take hold of that for which Christ once took hold of me. My friends, I do not reckon myself to have got hold of it yet. All I can say is this: forgetting what is behind me, and reaching out for that which lies ahead, I press towards the goal to win the prize which is God's call to the life above, in Christ Jesus (Phil. 3:12–14, NEB).

I spent the other day attempting to achieve some semblance of order out of the fifteen years of sermons I have on file—over three thousand of them!

I recall, once, in a homiletics class, a preacher friend of mine saying that he never saved his sermons. After hearing him preach I didn't blame him! After my trip through my file the other day, I joined him!

My First Sermon.—My first sermon was preached in 1955 in my father's pulpit on my mother's birthday! For thirty-five minutes I waxed strong and exhausted everything I ever knew and ever learned about any and everything!

My Most Controversial Sermon.—I had quite a time figuring out which one won this award, believe me! But the prize went to a sermon preached in 1959. The town in which I served in Kentucky had an annual Memorial Day service at the local cemetery, at the same time as our morning service, led by a fraternal order not particularly noted for its piety. I'd show 'em! I announced my subject: "Why I Will Not Go to the Cemetery." The only problem was that no one showed up to hear it—they all went to the cemetery!

My Worst Sermon.—This was a difficult decision! A little voice kept saying, "Last Sunday's was pretty close!" I thought it was the devil to be sure! But it was only my wife looking over my shoulder! No decision reached—it ended in a 3,000-way tie!

MY BEST SERMON. My best sermon! After hours of debate within myself, I have decided my best sermon is yet to be preached.

Renewal Reminder: *Remind me, O Lord, that my best sermon is the one I live. Amen.*

NOTES:

36.   Living an Ethic

"You are light for all the world. A town that stands on a hill cannot be hidden. When a lamp is lit, it is not put under the meal-tub, but on the lamp-stand, where it gives light to everyone in the house. And you, like the lamp, must shed light among your fellows, so that, when they see the good you do, they may give praise to your Father in heaven" (Matt. 5:14–16, NEB).

I saw a television program this week. A Western.

I was moved to tears.

With dramatic impact, a host of seasoned performers interacted around a plot which magnified a deed of real moral principle.

With deep conviction, amidst an emotionally charged atmosphere, people were portrayed doing something just because it was right to do it.

There it was, center stage, the dramatization of a superlative ethic.

It stimulated two thoughts.

First, wouldn't it be a wonderful world if everybody would do right!

Second, wouldn't it be a woeful world if everybody did wrong! If we all rebelled against the right; if we threw off all moral restraint—cheating, lying, stealing, plundering, rioting, murdering, embezzling, pilfering, and destroying.

No dull grey relativism in that program! A distinct difference was made between the right and the wrong. In this sense, it made one wish all television was in "black and white!"

Instead, so often, television is prostituted for the loose moral interests of a jaded society which smirks at any ennobling, moral theme.

Nevertheless, with or without the powerful influence of television, let the Christian church continue to be salt in this world, preserving it from all which would putrefy, constantly voicing the ethical precepts and principles that have kept American society fit to live in.

God help America without it!

Renewal Reminder: *Remind me, O Lord, to be a "white hat" today. Amen.*

NOTES:

37. Once When I Was a Church Member

"We ought to see how each of us may best arouse others to love and active goodness, not staying away from our meetings, as some do, but rather encouraging one another, all the more because you see the Day drawing near" (Heb. 10:24–25, NEB).

Sometimes I wonder if I was shortchanged in that I never had the opportunity of being an ordinary church member! Not only was I denied that ordinary status by being a PK (preacher's kid), but I was converted at the age of sixteen during the month of April, and by August of that same year, I had surrendered to the ministry and have preached nearly every Sunday since!

But once I was! It happened during seminary. I had gone from Kentucky to seminary in North Carolina without a pastorate or a place to preach. Not knowing a soul in North

Carolina, we began to look for a church home. After attending several churches in the area, we decided to join a church in Raleigh. We joined, quite frankly, because we liked the preacher. (That's not the best way to join a church, I know, but it's the method most of us use. It's rather frightening to a pastor, believe me!)

I learned some lessons during that brief experience of being a church member—lessons I've not forgotten. Chief among those lessons was that of learning what it is to attend and join a church where you don't know a soul! How much you want someone—anyone—to learn and call your name, to wave at you or even nod their head—and how seldom it happens!

Of all the fond memories I have of that church, the dearest is of a man who belonged to my Sunday School class who, after only one visit in Sunday School, knew my name and spoke to me. He was not a teacher, not a deacon—just a ''John-Doe-member.'' In all honesty, I used to look for him each Sunday just so I'd have someone to wave to, someone who knew me—and he always did! He will never know how much that meant.

Someone may be looking for you this Sunday. Don't fail him.

Renewal Reminder: *Remind me, O Lord, to watch for those who are watching and to need those who are needing. Amen.*

NOTES:

38.   The Things that Happen

They were all lost in amazement and praised God; filled with awe they said, "You would never believe the things we have seen today" (Luke 5:26, NEB).

One Sunday as I was preaching on Hebrews 12:1–4 ("Lest ye be wearied and faint") on the subject, "We Do Faint," when I was midway in the message a lady fainted! Nurses came, an ambulance was called, the whole works! The things that happen to me, you wouldn't believe!

I am just thankful that I did not preach a sermon on "We Do Die"! Although, now that I know I have this unique suggestive power, I plan soon to preach on "Awake, Thou That Sleepest!" The things that happen.

Then, there was that time in Knoxville, Tennessee, where as a ministerial student I preached each Saturday night in a skid-row mission. One night I was preaching on Jesus' trip to the Temple as a youth. When I said, "At the age of twelve," a drunk who was draped over a chair in the rear of the meeting place raised up long enough to say (in a voice that would pale a bull moose), "He was sixteen!" And, back to sleep he went! I don't think I have preached on that text since! The things that happen.

Once in a former pastorate we had a family who cared for foster children, often five or six at a time. I will never forget one little fellow they had, about five years old, who very evidently was in church for the first time in his life and very enamoured with it all. I was waxing eloquent saying, "Too long the church has been on the defensive! It's time we rose up from our trenches! It's time to sound the charge!" And, at the word "charge," the little fellow forgot himself and shouted out, "Bang!" Needless to say, that was the conclusion of the sermon!

Ah, you'd never believe the things that happen.

Renewal Reminder: *Remind me, O Lord, to expect the unexpected and the unexpected one: You. Amen.*

NOTES:

39. Sharing and Being Good News

*So with faith; if it does not lead to action,
it is in itself a lifeless thing. But someone
may object: "Here is one who claims to
have faith and another who points to his
deeds." To which I reply: "Prove to me
that this faith you speak of is real though
not accompanied by deeds, and by my
deeds I will prove to you my faith" (Jas.
2:17–18, NEB).*

Jesus came to both share the good news and
to be good news. It is our dual assignment,
too.

As we celebrate Christmas, exploring its
meaning, it is difficult to miss Christ's al-
legiance to both of these responsibilities. He
came to share the good news. It was the good
news that we are not alone. That God is
"pro-us," he is for us. He loves us. And, in
our sin, he has come to save us.

But, in the process of sharing this good
news, he was ever careful to be good news. To
the downtrodden, the overlooked, the out-
cast, the guilt-ridden, the broken—he, first,
was good news. In all of his dealings with
those like us, he was always considerate, loving, kind, and approachable.

Sad to say, some of his followers have not

always been so careful to maintain that balance. That is, we can be more than faithful in *sharing* the good news, but miss the equally important side of *being* good news. As I frequently say in conferences: "I know some people who share the good news who ain't!"

How do we merge the two? Well, as simple as it sounds, start with your face. What does your face say while you share the gospel? To illustrate what I mean, let me suggest that the next time you are watching a preacher on television, simply turn down the volume. See if his face communicates the good news. (The last one I saw looked pretty angry about something. When I turned up the volume, he was speaking on the love of God!) Then, try it in your own mirror!

People who were hungry for good news were irresistibly drawn to Jesus. A part of that magnetism had to do with his face, his manner. What he was seemed as important as what he said to the seekers. What he was able to say was, indeed, made possible because of what he was and how he said it.

In truth, ministry (being good news) is the flip side of evangelism (sharing good news).

If we are to see the church renewed in our time, we must include them both in a life-style like that of our Lord. It is a journey into both being and sharing good news to our world, not only our voices, but our faces and hands, as well.

Renewal Reminder: *Remind me, O Lord, to both "share" and "be" the good news today. Amen.*

NOTES:

40. What Would You Do?

*"Not everyone who calls me 'Lord, Lord'
will enter the kingdom of Heaven, but only
those who do the will of my heavenly
Father. When that day comes, many will
say to me, 'Lord, Lord, did we not prophesy in your name, cast out devils in your
name, and in your name perform many
miracles?' Then I will tell them to their
face, "I never knew you; out of my sight,
you and your wicked ways!"* (Matt.
7:21–23, NEB).

Every pastor begins to tremble a bit when
the next year's nominating committee is completed and elected, because he knows that
inevitably he will be confronted with their
questions—questions that put him on the spot
(or on the cross!).

You see, nominating committees have the
dastardly habit of asking the pastor questions
like these: "Did Mr. X do a good job with that
class?" "Did Mrs. Y attend committee meetings?" "Is it true that Mr. Z is uncooperative?"

And, almost as inevitable as are the questions is the fact that usually Mr. X is the cousin
of, Mrs. Y is the best friend of, and Mr. Z is
the father of one of the nominating committee
members!

So, the pastor's first reaction is to try to get
another engagement on the night of the committee meeting. But, he knows they will only
reschedule the meeting! He thinks long about

calling a constitution committee meeting and recommending that all nominating work be put under the responsibility of the minister of education. But, he discovers that the minister of education has already called such a meeting to ensure that it is kept under the responsibility of the pastor! So, he meets with them. Now, what would you recommend about:

A teacher who always goes home after Sunday School?

A committee member who hasn't attended a meeting?

A department which hasn't had one new member all year?

A member who has nothing but complaints?

A worker who is absent 50 percent of the time?

See what I mean?

While the majority always do a splendid, faithful job, there are always those few who make nominating committee time like a ride through Ulcer Gulch. So, if by chance one of the committee asks you, please tell them that you haven't seen the pastor!

Renewal Reminder: *Remind me, O Lord, that I am to do what you want me to do. Amen.*

41. What a Day It Was!

And I am sure that God who began the good work within you will keep right on helping you grow in his grace until his task within you is finally finished on that day when Jesus Christ returns (Phil. 1:6, TLB).

Sunday had been one of the highlights of my ministry, and at the Monday morning pastor's fellowship, all I could say was, "What a day it was!"

Coming to Sunday School I noted that the parking lots were full, but there was not a car parked near the buildings. Every one of those spaces had been left for visitors and latecomers!

During Sunday School the superintendent

stuck his head in the study door and was unable to contain himself: every teacher and superintendent was present, every department had reported visits made, and 98 percent had been on time.

Between Sunday School and worship the deacons gathered in the study to pray with the pastor and, with the exception of those involved in the choir and in ushering, every deacon was present! They encircled the pastor on the way to the church to protect him from those with little pieces of paper in their hands—last minute announcements that "have" to be made. Entering the choir room was a thrill! The choir director was aglow and said that every choir member was present and had been to rehearsal that week!

Upon entering the sanctuary I was struck by the noticeable silence. All over, heads were bowed. The singing was a delight to hear, even though it was a "new hymn." During the announcements I couldn't help but notice that the parents of those few teenagers who sometimes talk during the worship service were seated with them. When the Scripture lesson was announced, I had to delay an additional moment for so many were turning to read, also. The attentiveness during the message was sheer glory and so many came to greet the new members! As I made my way to the door during the choral benediction, I did not see a person putting on a coat! The social hall was jammed for the fellowship following the service. Families and friends were meeting and so many were talking to the visitors. The hostess came to say that they had run out of coffee because they had not expected so many!

So, you see why I said, "What a day it was!"
And, then, I woke up!

Renewal Reminder: *Remind me, O Lord, to make dreams come true today, your dreams for me. Amen.*

NOTES:

42.   Ever Old—Never New

*What has happened will happen again,
and what has been done will be done
again, and there is nothing new under
the sun. Is there anything of which one
can say, "Look this is new"? No, it has
already existed, long ago before our time
(Eccl. 1:9–10, NEB).*

The wisdom of "the preacher" in Ecclesiastes is apparent in his statement, "There is nothing new under the sun." With keen, but facetious insight, a friend of mine adds, "The only original thing about any of us is Original Sin!"

To illustrate, I read a book the other day entitled *Preaching in a Scientific Age*. The author said that there are four characteristics of contemporary congregations: (1) They are smaller in number; (2) They are less homogeneous in respect to their theology; (3) There is an ignorance and uncertainty of the Bible; and (4) They believe in science. Sound contemporary? It was written twenty five years ago!

To add insult to injury, let me quote a poem that I recently clipped from *Saturday Review*. It is written in the contemporary free verse style.

"To whom can I speak today? The gentle man has perished,
    The violent man has access to every-

body . . .

To whom can I speak today? There are no righteous men,

The earth is surrendered to criminals."

Though it sounds like someone who has his finger on the pulse of humanity today, it was written 4,000 years ago during Egypt's Middle Kingdom!

Nothing new! Every generation is dealt the same set of problems. Though the manifestations of the problems vary, the problems never do. They all stem from man's inherent bent of injustice to his fellowman. Whether history be cyclical or linear, the same set of problems is dealt to every set of men.

Yet, as Elton Trueblood says, "We are not responsible for the hand that is dealt to us; we are only responsible for how we play it."

Renewal Reminder: *Remind me, O Lord, that nothing is as old or as new as you. Amen.*

NOTES:

43. What Does the Preacher Do All Day?

He who descended is no other than he who ascended far above all heavens, so that he might fill the universe. And these were his gifts: some to be apostles, some prophets, some evangelists, some pastors and teachers, to equip God's people for work in his service, to the building up of the body of Christ (Eph. 4:11–12, NEB).

Ever hear that question? The strange thing is that although it is often asked about all pastors, it is never addressed to the pastor himself! Not only is it never asked of him, he never asks it of himself. His question is, "What should the pastor do?"

The basic problem of those who serve in this exciting last quarter of the twentieth century has to do with *function*: Just what is the pastor called to do? The teacher does not ask it—he is to teach. The singer doesn't have to ask it, nor the evangelist, nor the denominational employee. But, the pastor must.

The problem is further complicated by the fact that each of those whom the pastor serves has a differing concept of what he is to do and be. While they may wonder what he does, they do not wonder about what he should do—they know that! The problem is that everyone has something different in mind! There are those who see him primarily as a visitor of the members. Others see him as a counselor; others, as a personal evangelist, or administrator, or just plain preacher. Most, however, see him as *all* of these, but each has a different list of priorities about which is the most important! Consequently, no matter which way he goes, he invariably is a disappointment to some, if not most!

The only solution (and preventive for ulcers) is for the pastor to reach a clear concept of what God wants him to do and be, and then do it and be it, without regard save for him. He searchingly scours the Scriptures, he seeks the face of God in secret places, he views the burdens of his community, he listens for the heartbeat of his flock, and finally he hears "That Voice" and "Those Words" and responds. He chooses Christ's way as his way.

The more discerning viewers today are seeing that the pastor's primary call is to equip the members to do the work of the ministry, believing that all of us are ministers and that, by equipping the members, he can multiply himself and be all of those things through them.

It is the difference in merely counting for Christ and multiplying for him!

Renewal Reminder: *Remind me, O Lord, to be all you want **me** to be and to help others to be all you want them to be, too. Amen.*

NOTES:

44. On Rededicating Your Life

Restore to me again the joy of your salvation, and make me willing to obey you. Then I will teach your ways to other sinners, and they—guilty like me—will repent and return to you (Ps. 51:12–13, TLB).

There are times in our Christian experience when actions, attitudes, or animosities enter our lives and a rededication becomes necessary. Whether the move is prompted by the presence of wrong or the absence of right, such a serious decision demands full awareness of what is involved. With a pastor's heart, I share some things about rededication which might be helpful to all of us.

Rededication has, not only a backward, but also a forward look. To be sure, rededication should seek forgiveness for past failure. But don't stop there. Primarily, rededication has a forward look; that is, it looks toward the future with determination not only to be forgiven, but to be better. (Often when one comes in rededication I ask if their decision means they are going to begin attending Sunday School or tithing or visiting.) Rededication is an empty formality if one does not emerge a more active member of Christ's church.

Rededication has, not only a general, but also a specific look. In rededication, every area of life should be examined and recommitted to the Lord. Most often, however, it is the one specific failure which creates the sense of need to rededicate. Be brutally specific—what has caused the sense of guilt? And then, not only seek forgiveness; get the victory over it! The only way to do this is to get it out in the open before the Lord, tell him what it is, ask for victory over it, and leave believing that he will avail all the power of heaven to you for the battle.

Rededication has, not only an emotional, but also a volitional look. We often come forward in tears saying that we want to rededicate our lives. My counsel is usually, "Then, why don't you do it?" Wanting and doing are two different things. Rededication must be a decision, not just a desire, if it is to be meaningful. It should be as definite a decision as conversion itself. The way to do this is to tell the Lord, not that you want to, but that you are rededicating your life. Then your decision takes on a definite quality.

And, who of us does not need it?

Renewal Reminder: *Remind me, O Lord, to rededicate myself today for today. Amen.*

NOTES:

45. A Matter of Orientation to New Members
(Not taught in the New Member's Class)

*A soft answer turns away wrath, but
harsh words cause quarrels (Prov. 15:1,
TLB).*

It is common knowledge within Christendom about feudin' Baptists. It just seems that one can't be a Baptist of any worth unless he has a fussin' ability. And, it is true! But, don't misunderstand.

Thus, as a matter of orientation to new Baptists (and as a matter of explanation to any chance reader from a more composed communion), let me explain this Baptist phenomenon. Yes sir, we are the fussin' variety.

But, don't be fooled!

A Baptist church is like a family. We can fuss about and with our own with no holds barred, but let an outsider do it and watch what happens! We can knock each other about twenty-five hours a day, but let trouble come and see the response!

Baptist preachers, in disagreement over policy, have been known to do bloody battle on a convention floor and leave the convention hall arm-in-arm. No sir, don't be fooled about Baptist solidarity! Church members, locked in mortal combat on Sunday, have been seen on Monday visiting an unsaved person together. No sir, don't be fooled!

To be sure, there are a few Baptists who misunderstand this healthy glandular activity for dislike or hatred. They usually break the one ground rule of Baptist battling: keeping the battle within the family. But, these are just unseasoned recruits who soon learn after a few skirmishes.

Is there any evidence of the truth of this? Yes sir! In the midst of all the fussin', witness a Baptist church family. Just watch the long line of happy members who welcome a new member! Just listen to the laughter in the aisles after any service has been dismissed. No sir, don't be fooled!

Baptists are activists and when there is a lull, our recreational demeanor demands a fuss. But don't confuse Baptist athletics for animosity!

So then, my fellow member, you don't like what I do? Well, just roll up your sleeves, stick out your fist, and shake! I'm one of us!

Renewal Reminder: *Remind me, O Lord, that what I do reveals what I am. Amen.*

NOTES:

46.   Chains and the Bible

Nothing is perfect except your words.
Oh, how I love them. I think about them
all day long. They make me wiser than
my enemies, because they are my constant
guide. Yes, wiser than my teachers, for I
am ever thinking of your rules. They
make me even wiser than the aged (Ps.
119:96–100, TLB).

When privileged to preach in another pulpit, more often than not, I arrive behind the sacred desk to discover on the lectern a pulpit Bible. Frankly, my first impulse is to pick it up and put it away!

Pulpit Bibles have a long history. The concept dates back to the latter part of the Dark Ages. During that period Bibles were taboo for the laity; that is, the ordinary lay Christian was not permitted to own or to read the Bible. Most often, the only Bible in the community was the pulpit Bible. But it was not like our contemporary pulpit Bibles. It was chained to the pulpit, with a lock on it, to be read only by the priest-pastor! Thus, every time I see one, I shudder to think of the day when the Word was denied the people. Bibles don't belong on the pulpit! They belong in the hands of the people!

The tragedy, however, is that for all practical purposes the Bible is still chained to the pulpit! That is, it is still a book that only the pastor reads. A recent survey revealed that only 12 percent of those who say they believe the Bible actually read it every day; 34 percent read it only once a week; and 42 percent read only once in a long while!

Let's become a Bible-reading people! In the Sunday School class, use your Bible to read the Scripture portion. The pastor's Scripture lesson ought to be printed in the bulletin so that the congregation can locate it early in the service and follow the reading in their own Bibles. Families should set aside a time to read the Bible.

Read your Bible daily in private devotions. Study it. Hide it in your heart. And then be a doer of the Word.

Today, if there be any chains on the Bible, let them be of our hearts!

Renewal Reminder: *Remind me, O Lord, to hide your Word in my heart today for today and tomorrow. Amen.*

NOTES:

47. Some "Remarkable" Church Practices

Again I looked throughout the earth and saw that the swiftest person does not always win the race, nor the strongest man the battle, and that wise men are often poor, and skillful men are not necessarily famous; but it is all by chance, by happening to be at the right place at the right time (Eccl. 9:11, TLB).

One of the things I learned from Dr. George W. Redding, professor of religion at Georgetown College, Kentucky, was the proper use of the word *remarkable*. To say that something is remarkable is to say that "all sorts of remarks" could be made about it!

Now, here are some remarkable church practices.

There is a Baptist church in Tennessee

whose pastor mimeographs his sermons during the week before he preaches them on Sunday. Then, after Sunday School, he goes to the parking lot to distribute them to those who are sneaking away! Remarkable!

In the early New England churches, ushers did not take the offering. Indeed, their function was to prowl the aisles during the sermon with long poles in hand to punch those who had fallen asleep during two-hour sermons! Remarkable!

At the end of each year, a large black Baptist church in Texas prints the names of all members and their total contributions for the year for churchwide distribution. The list begins with the pastor, the deacons, and then every member! Remarkable!

There is a small church in Washington, D.C., which requires every member to witness weekly and report on it publicly, to tithe, and to attend weekly Bible study and worship—or be dropped from membership! Remarkable!

Another Texas Baptist church is giving S & H Green stamps to everyone attending evening services and attendance is continuing to climb! Remarkable!

A Louisville-area church takes no offering during the worship services because, according to the pastor, all members attend the Sunday School and give their tithes there! Remarkable!

In fact, aren't we all rather remarkable?

Renewal Reminder: *Remind me, O Lord, that you called me to a remarkable life. Amen.*

NOTES:

48. The Moon Shots and the Greatness of Man

From the end of the earth will I cry unto thee, when my heart is overwhelmed: lead me to the rock that is higher than I (Ps. 61:2).

The greatness of man, that which separates him from all else in God's creation and which is his uniqueness and glory, is not that he made it to the moon—but that he wanted to go! There is that in man which impulsively and instinctively seeks horizons.

"Does man belong on the moon?" That incisive, single question has two equally true and equally contradictory answers. On one hand, some ask, "If not, why did God put it there?" (I can almost hear Adam ask that of the apple in the Garden!) On the other hand, some say, "We are not to be there because God made man to have dominion over the earth, not the moon." (But, then, why the insatiable explorative urge in man, seeing God made him that way?) So, the question, "Does man belong on the moon?" has two answers, then, equally true and mutually exclusive; hence, it has no answer! It must be filed, then, along with Cain's wife; the chicken and the egg; and the author of the book of Hebrews.

And, it remains: Man's glory is not so much that he made it to the moon, but that he wanted to go!

But, oh, that we could turn that insatiable explorative urge inward—toward (and over) the horizons of the heart! That we could touch down on the sea of tranquility and set out for the center of the soul! That, en route, we could climb the heights of the self's heart, view the purgative, white-hot issue of the volcano of light, rest awhile on the rock, search out the hiding places of God within, and ultimately find that Paradise which God himself has surveyed, cleared, and planted for us in the soul's center where awaits a holy supper of living bread and water for the travel-weary sojourners of the soul. And . . .

Your greatness, fellow stranger, will not be that you make it there—if you ever do; but, rather, that you wanted to go! And, by the way, a tour is leaving this Sunday at your church!

Renewal Reminder: *Remind me, O Lord, that my journey inward and my journey outward should precede my journey upward. Amen.*

NOTES:

49.   0123456789

I count everything sheer loss, because all is far outweighed by the gain of knowing Christ Jesus my Lord, for whose sake I did in fact lose everything. I count it so much garbage, for the sake of gaining Christ and finding myself incorporate in him, with no righteousness of my own, no legal rectitude, but the righteousness which comes from faith in Christ, given by God in response to faith. All I care for is to know Christ, to experience the power of his resurrection, and to share his sufferings, in growing conformity with his death, if only I may finally arrive at the resurrection from the dead (Phil. 3:8–11, NEB).

Plagued with numbers! Since kindergarten days with my learning "One little, two little, three little Indians," it has been numbers, numbers, numbers!

To the government, the finance company, auto license bureau, the insurance company, I am but a number. It is getting so I can't even pick up the telephone without hearing "Number, please." And, then, the zip code!

I thought surely I would escape the plague at college, but even they had my number—zero! After college, seeking a job to pay off my numerous academic debts, I was hired as a junior high school teacher of, you guessed it, math!

I can't even escape it at home. Driving up to number 207 the other day, I was met by my wife, a pretty number herself, with the words, "Hello, Number One." I still don't know if she was referring to my place in her life or to the fact that her lean 140-pound lover resembles a number one!

Surely, I thought, escape could be found at church. Then I heard the choir director say, "Welcome! Let's begin the worship by turning to Number . . . ."! It was too much! Beating a retreat to my study, I knew the Lord would name instead of number me. Seeking a word of consolation, I let the Bible fall open and looked. Oh no! . . . the book of NUMBERS! Even the Lord must be against me!

Beloved, I'm numb with numbers!

Numb, but not dumb. Numbers are here to stay. Let's make the best of a bad thing. I suggest (and all this is just to say the following) that for Christians: number one among days be the Lord's Day; number one among books be the Bible; number one among institutions be the church; number one among dollars be the tithe; and number one among persons be the person of Jesus.

And, I can't help but add, churches can't count zeros. Why not be one of the countable numbers this Sunday? If you are not countable, then someone has your number!

Renewal Reminder: *Remind me, O Lord, to be*

so accountable that I can always be countable. Amen.

NOTES:

50. Actions: Louder Than Words and Reactions Even Louder!

Let your bearing towards one another arise out of your life in Christ Jesus (Phil. 2:5, NEB).

That actions speak louder than words and that actions tend to identify us is more or less true.

But, it is not a foolproof method. Christians often do wrong and non-Christians very often do good! Thus, to say that a person's Christianity (or lack of it) is indicated by his actions is not wholly true. But, it is at least a part of the evidence!

Even more indicative, however, than our actions are our reactions. This is true, you see, because we can calculate and plan our actions in advance, but not our reactions. Reactions catch us off guard.

For instance: We plan to do a good deed (action) for someone. Much to our surprise, however, the recipient of our good deed rejects it and curses us for it without our expecting such. Now, our reactions will be more indicative of the depth of Christianity in us than the action itself!

It's always those spur-of-the-moment reactions that get us! Suddenly, without expectation or foreknowledge, someone caustically criticizes us, severely hurts us, introduces something to which we are violently opposed, and our normal, calculated sweet spirit is shattered! And, we react!

What is the secret to Christian reactions? The secret is a life continually centered on and in Christ. It is the abdicated life, to the control of the Spirit. Otherwise, our lives are spasmodic and irregular and inconsistent.

How does one gain that abdicated life? How does one live under the continual sway and control of Christ? While it is not the whole answer, 99 percent of it is a devotional life! Prayer—that is communion with God. Bible reading—that is communion with God. Meditation—that is communion with God.

Equally crucial to the abdicated life is a worship life which, also, is communion with God. And the more consistent we are in these matters of prayer, Bible reading, meditation, and worship, the more consistent we will be in our reactions.

Renewal Reminder: *Remind me, O Lord, to be so close to you that even my reactions reflect you. Amen.*

NOTES:

51.   Does the Spirit Lead?

For as many as are led by the Spirit of
God, they are the sons of God (Rom.
8:14).

Of this I am convinced: that the Holy Spirit
of God is always at work in our world, at work
on the hearts of men and women, convicting
and convincing them of their need for God. I
am equally convinced of another Spirit fact,
too: that he who is the preparer of hearts is
also the prompter of hearts. That is, when a
convicted soul reaches his or her moment of
truth, the resident Spirit moves in the heart of
some believer and he is prompted to speak to
the prepared soul in need. He brings their

paths to cross! But only the spiritually sensitive ever know it.

As I hurriedly drove to the hospital, late already, I passed by the home of one whom I knew to be seeking. I was deeply impressed to stop, and I did, even though it would only make me more late. When the door opened, my friend stood with tear-filled eyes and said, "I want to become a Christian."

Funny, but I hadn't thought of another friend for months, but I felt greatly inclined to pick up the telephone, though the call would be halfway across the country. I did. Their home and marriage had just exploded and there had been no one to help them. "How did you know?," I was asked.

It was late, nearly 10:00 P.M., as I was driving home from several visits. I knew, or at least I thought, that I ought to make another call—a specific one. But, it was late. And, I was tired—really tired. I would do it tomorrow. When I arrived home, the telephone rang. Yes, it was . . .

Is this a special gift? You bet it is! It belongs only to a chosen few. We call them Christians! They are those who have given their hearts and lives to Christ with a vow to ever be at his disposal. The Holy Spirit resides in them and takes them at their word about being "available." He will lead the lead-able.

Renewal Reminder: *Remind me, O Lord, to be lead-able today. Amen.*

NOTES:

52. What Is Christianity Worth to Mankind?

For God so loved the world, that he gave his only begotten Son, that whosoever believeth in him should not perish, but have everlasting life (John 3:16).

Just recently I received a card from a friend. It was brief and to the point. It asked six brief questions: "What has Christianity done for mankind? What for our world? What for our nation? What for our town? What for you?

What will Christianity be worth to man when Christ returns?" For whatever it is worth, here is my answer.

I received your card with the questions on it. I confess I don't know quite what you mean. Is it just a thought or are you asking me for answers? Let me say this, friend, in a sense you are asking a wrong question: like, "Do you still beat your wife?" That's a wrong question because it assumes something which may or may not be true. The question of the worth of Christianity to mankind is a wrong question because it puts worth on the wrong end! Whether or not it is worth anything at all to man, now or whenever, does not for a moment change its worth. The question is—what is it worth to God and to Christ?

For instance, an ignorant savage could find a diamond or a gold ingot or a dollar bill. It may not be worth anything to him, but that doesn't change its worth, does it? Whether man ever accepts Christianity or uses it does not affect its worth in the least; it may be unemployed worth, but it is still worth.

From God's standpoint it was worth his Son, the birth of the King in a stable, death on a cross, and much more. That's the answer to its worth, and the only answer. Ultimately, too, the worth of Christianity is always personal. The question is not mankind, but, to you. Whether anybody else thinks it is worth all, or worthless, makes no real difference.

Personally, it is worth my life or I would not be in the pulpit on Sundays or on the streets during the week.

I share this with you because, while it is not a valid question, it is nonetheless being asked by many today. How would, how do, you answer it?

Renewal Reminder: *Remind me, O Lord, that you alone are worthy, not I. Amen.*

NOTES:

53. The Weakest Link

And whether one member suffer, all the
members suffer with it; or one member be
honoured, all the members rejoice with it
(1 Cor. 12:26).

The proverb goes: "A chain is only as strong
as its weakest link." I've heard it over and
over again. In fact, I read it just the other day.
And very often it is applied to the church.
Now, however, let me respond to it. Phooey!

That's right! "A church is only as strong as
its weakest member." Phooey! If this is so,
churches are in big trouble—if they are only as
strong as their weakest member!

If we are only as strong as our weakest
member (and, actually it should be plural—
weakest members—for about one third of all
believers are obviously in a race for the title),
then we would never have a Sunday School
class or a worship service. It it were so, we
would never give a penny to missions or a
needy family. If so, we wouldn't even have a
church staff, a youth program or a building.
No hymnals, no bulletins, no anything! No
prayer would ever be offered for the sick, the
pastor, or the unchurched. No deacons would
visit troubled families because, if we were
only as strong as our weakest member, no one
would be spiritually qualified to be a deacon!

That's why I say phooey! A theological, apocalyptic, existential, eschatological, and ecclesiastical phooey! And, you can quote me on that.

But, the converse is not true, either. That is, that we are as strong as our strongest member. There are a precious few among us whose Christlikeness is praiseworthy. The bald truth is that we are as strong, or as weak, as our pooled assets and lives. Some bring more in terms of money and talents because they have more. The standard is not how much, but how well in light of how much. And, even the best among us is not operating at optimum!

All of this is to say that all of us need to be stronger links than we are!

Renewal Reminder: *Remind me, O Lord, that my strength comes from you, not me or my efforts. Amen.*

NOTES:

54.   What Happened?

*Ye did run well; who did hinder you that
ye should not obey the truth? (Gal. 5:7).*

"What happened to the church in Western
Europe?" Two hundred years ago, it was the
spiritual center of gravity for world Christianity. Two hundred years ago, they were sending the missionaries—some of them to
America; they were writing the theology
books; they were reaching the people. Two
hundred years ago, they represented the new
and the fresh and the vibrant.

Now, two hundred years later, the spiritual
center of gravity has moved to North America
and the institutional church in Western
Europe is all but dead. In some places only 20
percent of the population attends the church
services. What happened?

I spent a month in Western Europe not long
ago trying to find some causes. I felt that it
was important to know because North American Christianity has usually followed the pat-

tern of Europe with regularity. About fifty years later we usually do the same as they have done. Not surprisingly, then, our attendance is now dropping from a high of 50 percent down to a present 37 percent, according to the latest Gallup poll. If we could know what trends they followed, perhaps it would be of help to us as we seek to avert it.

Some of the reasons are peculiarly European due to the state church situation there, being financed through tax monies, and to the theological development of the past. But most of the reasons for their decline are applicable here. Let me share what I heard and saw:

1. *The church became dominated by the clergy.*—Whether this was an abdication by the laity or a domination by the clergy is not always clear. But, whichever, it resulted in a minority doing it for the church. This is a curious reversal in the cradle of the Reformation whose rallying cry was the priesthood of the believer.

2. *The church became biblically illiterate.*— Theological trends changed rapidly in Europe and the leaders seemed to buy each new idea. The more they changed, the more the people became disillusioned with all of it. Not having a strong Bible-teaching approach, the people had no defense. They were not equipped to distinguish in doctrinal areas.

3. *The church became an audience rather than a family.*—As the trends developed, the people became satisfied merely to show up for the

services. They lost not only their relationship to Christ, but more so, their relationship to each other as the family of God. They became members of an institution but not of each other. They settled for periodic parties and socials, calling them fellowships.

Could it be, that, again, we are going to follow the trends set in Western Europe? Or, will we accept the challenge to renew the church? As yet, it remains to be seen.

Renewal Reminder: *Remind me, O Lord, that I am to be a part of the solution, not of the problem. Amen.*

NOTES:

55. Captive Churches

And it shall come to pass in the last days,
saith God, I will pour out of my Spirit
upon all flesh: and your sons and your
daughters shall prophesy, and your
young men shall see visions, and your old
men shall dream dreams (Acts 2:17).

I had a dream the other night, a horrible
dream. I guess that I dreamed about it because
I had been thinking so much about the issue
around which it focused—"The cultural captivity of our Christianity." Whether we an-
nounce it or not, we many times require a
person to adapt to our culture before he or she
can be adopted into our church families.

But, back to that dream. It was about a
church which, for some reason, found all of its
deacons were teenagers! When the teenagers
discovered it, things really began to happen.

First, they changed the format of the worship services. A major move was that they
voted to use the organ only at special services,
and then only on Sunday nights. Instead,
they voted to use guitars and drums.

Then, they voted to do away with the hym-
nal in preference to the newer youth songs.
Their reasoning? They did not like the other
music; it wasn't appropriate.

Of course, the adults objected, but the
youth leaders were firm: "All of us are going

to worship alike or else!"

Because of Wednesday night ball games at school, they moved prayer meeting to Thursday night. Their reasoning was that church services ought to be conveniently scheduled. That the adults had civic club and fraternal meetings on Thursdays made little difference to them. They simply replied: "You'll just have to choose which is more important."

Another major move came later. They began to chide the adults about their wearing apparel and general appearance. No vote was taken, of course, but pressure was placed on the adults about wearing double knits and short hair. It just wasn't becoming. In our church, they said, wear jeans and long hair. Anything else is out of place.

The adults, however, began to react to all of this. First, several quit coming. The youth replied, "We just don't know what's gotten into the older generation: they just aren't interested in the things of the Lord." It wasn't a lament as much as it was an explanation.

Other adults, however, stuck it out. Finally, they organized a separate adult program and asked for an adult director. The Youth Board took it under advisement, but dragged on and on with it, never making a recommendation.

Next, the adult group asked for a separate adult service while the youth were in prayer meeting. But, they were turned down because, the youth said, "We need to worship together as a whole church." Any adult activities, they said, would have to be in addition to the existing program.

It wasn't long, however, until more and more adults began to drop out. Some went to a neighboring church because they had a good adult program. The youth discounted this as but a passing fad or phase. "They'll be back," the youth said.

But, they didn't come back. In fact, others left until there were no adults at all! Admittedly, everyone at church now looked, talked, sang, and worshiped alike, but, there were no adults. Which was better?

Yes, it was a horrible dream—"The cultural captivity of our Christianity." I woke up, but I still think about it. I hope you do, too!

Renewal Reminder: *Remind me, O Lord, that it is time to be awake. Amen.*

NOTES:

56. A Holy Hum

And he spake a parable unto them to this
end, that men ought always to pray, and
not to faint (Luke 18:1).

I had heard it expressed in other terms, but
never so succinctly as by R. Eugene Sterner
who said: "The church is called to be *holy*
before it is called to *hum*."

In his book, *Being the Community of Christian
Love,* Sterner adds, "We are indeed called to
do, but we are first called to be." Our very
activism, he says, "may be a cover-up for the
spiritual poverty we feel."

There is a growing awareness that a hurricane of Christian activity, like any hurricane,
can have a vacuum at its center. One of the
things I repeatedly saw as a pastor was that
some of my busiest members were frequently
some of my shallowest members. And, why?

Perhaps, it is a conditioned response we
have learned. That is, when we realize that we
are out of step with God, our first response
toward correcting it is to get busy at something in the church. But, alas, busyness does

not correct it. A relational problem is not solved by a functional change! Consequently, we often get busier. When that fails to satisfy, we just keep adding more and more jobs in the church.

As a pastor I even helped to condition this response for a good part of my ministry. That is, I actually counseled people to get busy in the church as a corrective to spiritual emptiness. I even initiated this conditioned response in the lives of new Christians by immediately giving them a job when what they really needed was to be grounded in faith!

It is this same misunderstanding which prompts a few with limited spiritual grasp to criticize prayer and Bible study groups. Usually the comment is that they don't do anything. Maybe these strugglers realize, better than their leaders, the necessity of *being* before *doing.* Leave them at it awhile. People cannot linger near the Lord, in prayer and the Word, without sooner or later doing something.

This is not to say that inactivity is a symptom of maturity. Not by any means! As Elton Trueblood has said, "Jesus called for laborers, not admirers." But, it is to say that roots must precede fruits.

Whenever and wherever we talk of the renewal of the church and the Christian, we must start at the right place—the inner life. It is out of the heart from which the issues of life proceed. Being and doing are mates, but in that order. This means that our real goal is not merely to be holy or to hum, but rather to seek a holy hum in our churches and in our lives. And, that's genuine renewal!

Renewal Reminder: *Remind me, O Lord, that holiness is my calling. Amen.*

NOTES:

57. God, Golf, and Guff

A happy face means a glad heart (Prov. 15:13, TLB).

Being both a golfer, of the duffer category, and a preacher makes for a lot of guff, believe you me! Indeed, some feel that it is wholly unholy for a holy man to try to hole it! But, to clear the air and set the record straight, let it be known that golf is wholly holy Scripture!

(The reader will note that the passages of Scripture are taken out of context.)

It is written, "Provide yourselves bags" (Luke 12:33), "Whether there be wood therein or not" (Num. 13:20). "Moreover take thou unto thee an iron" (Ezek. 4:3). There, you see? scriptural!

Why, just the other day as I was hooking and slicing my way up a less-than-fair fairway, I had occasion to think of Job 10:15, "Yet will I not lift up my head!" And, after losing a ball or two I could faithfully speak, "He hears not the shouts of the driver. . . . He searches after every green thing" (Job 39:7–8, RSV) and "All the pins thereof . . ." (Ex. 27:19).

In addition to all the hooks and slices and lost balls, I found myself going from sand trap to sand trap! I scripturally lamented: "They set a trap; they catch men, like a basket full of birds'' (Jer. 5:26–27, RSV). Having blown hole after hole, I had no alternative but to admit, "Their course is evil" (Jer. 23:10).

I refuse to tell you my score, but I can tell you in the words of Zechariah the prophet: "I took two staffs; one I named Grace, and the other I named Union. And I took my staff Grace, and I broke it. Then I broke my second staff Union" (11:7,10,14, RSV). And, with gritted teeth and clenched fist I asked in a shout, "Can one break iron?" (Jer. 15:12, RSV).

Dr. Jess Moody says, "If a minister shoots a high score, he is neglecting his golf; if he shoots a low one, he is neglecting his church!" Either way, the preacher is a perennial loser!

Renewal Reminder: *Remind me, O Lord, that I'm always a loser apart from you. Amen.*

NOTES:

NOTES:

NOTES:

NOTES:

NOTES:

NOTES:

NOTES:

NOTES:

NOTES: